Hallelujah
and Other Songs of Inspiration

T0079205

ISBN 978-1-4803-4448-8

HAL•LEONARD®
CORPORATION

7777 W. BLUEMOUND RD. P.O. BOX 13819 MILWAUKEE, WI 53213

Visit Hal Leonard Online at
www.halleonard.com

Amazing Grace

Words by John Newton
Traditional American Melody

Duet Part (Student plays one octave higher than written.)

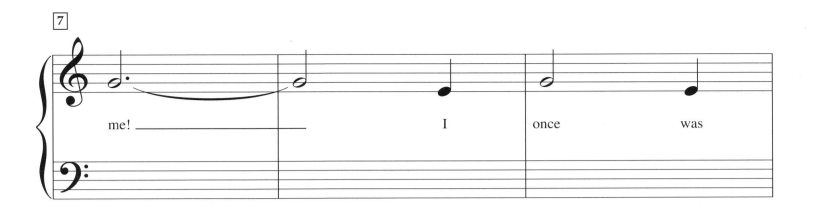

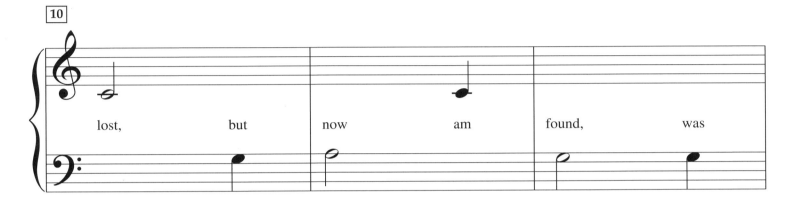

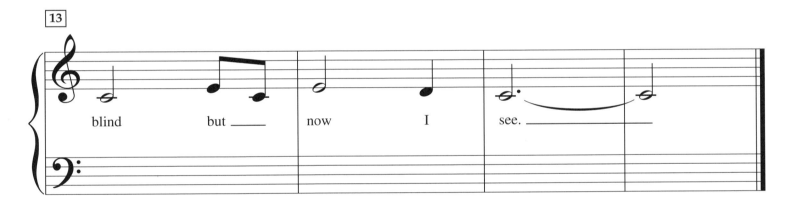

3

Circle of Life
from Walt Disney Pictures' THE LION KING

Music by Elton John
Lyrics by Tim Rice

Duet Part (Student plays one octave higher than written.)

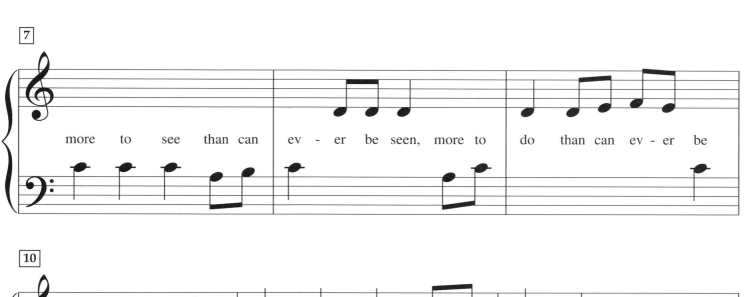

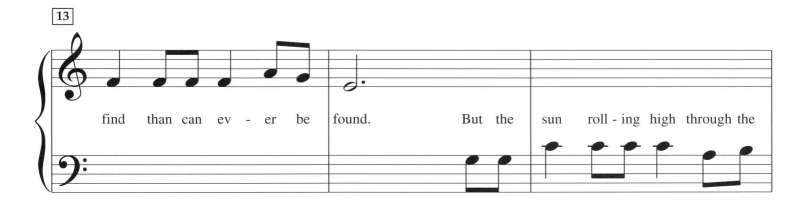

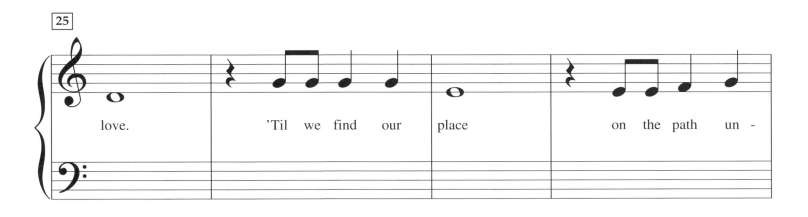

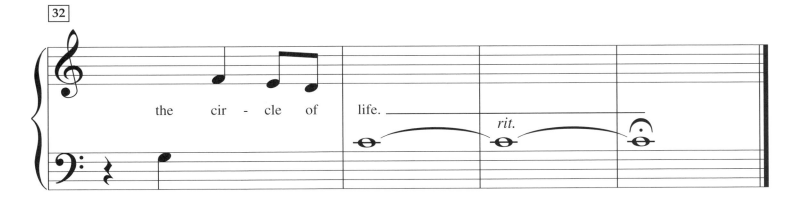

People Got to Be Free

Words and Music by FELIX CAVALIERE
and EDWARD BRIGATI, JR.

Duet Part (Student plays one octave higher than written.)

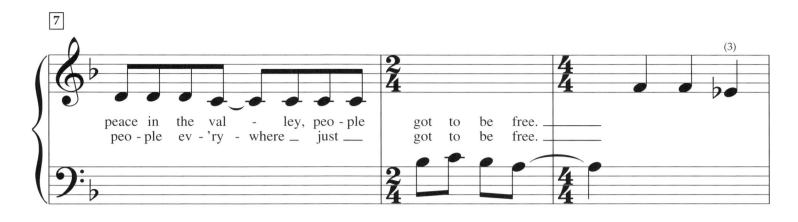

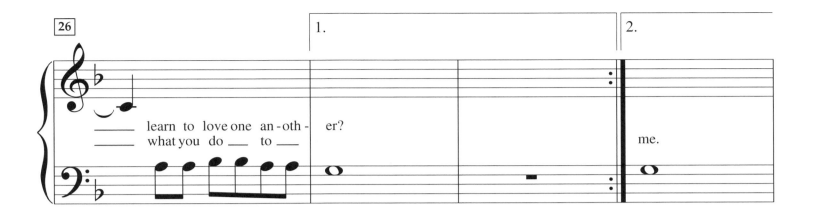

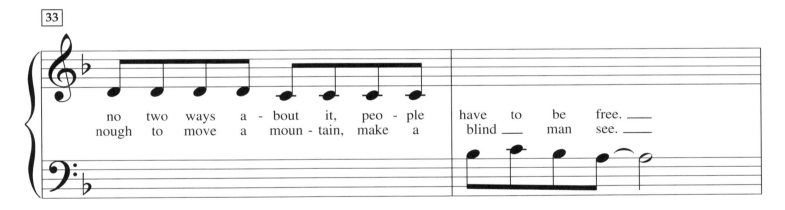

Ask me my o - pin - ion, my o - pin - ion will be, _____ it's a
Ev - 'ry - bod - y's danc - in', come on, let's ___ go see. _____ There's _

nat - 'ral sit - u - a - tion for a man to be free. _____
peace _ in the val - ley, now we all can be free. _____

12

Don't Stop Believin'

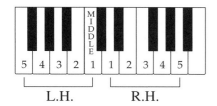

Words and Music by Steve Perry,
Neal Schon and Jonathan Cain

Moderately fast, in 2

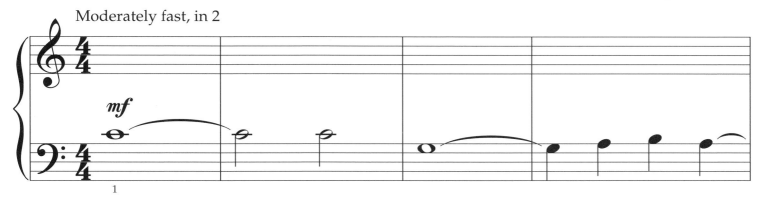

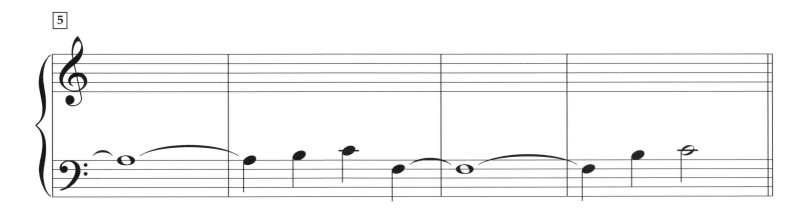

Duet Part (Student plays one octave higher than written.)

Moderately fast, in 2

an - y - where.
an - y - where.

on   and   on _____   and   on _____   and   on. _____

Stran - gers _____   wait - ing _____
Street - light _____   peo - ple, _____

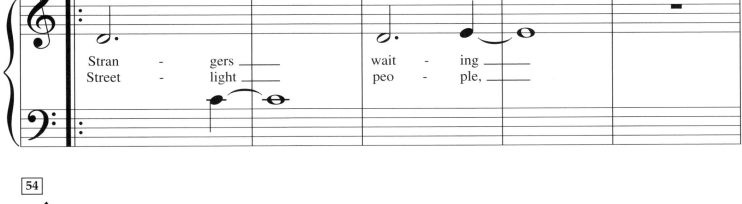

up   and   down   the   boul - e - vard, _____   their   shad - ows __
liv - ing   just   to   find   e - mo - tion,   hid - ing __

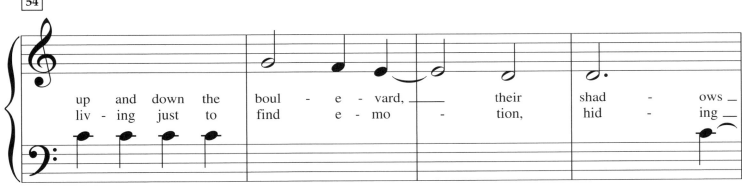

Hold on to the feel - in', _____

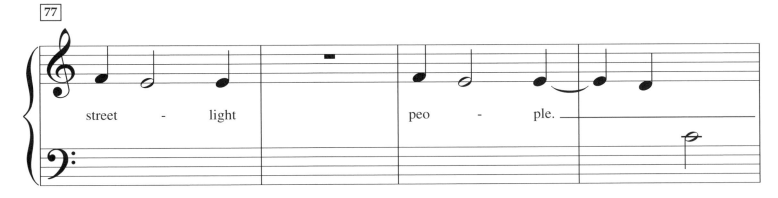

street - light peo - ple. _____

Don't _____ stop!

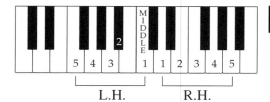

Hallelujah

Words and Music by
LEONARD COHEN

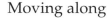

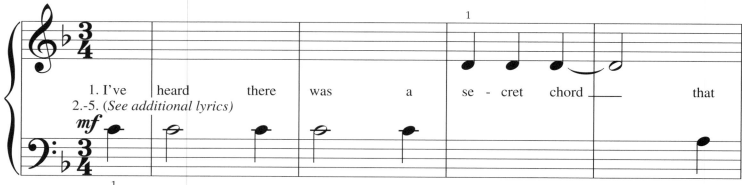

Moving along

1. I've heard there was a se - cret chord ____ that

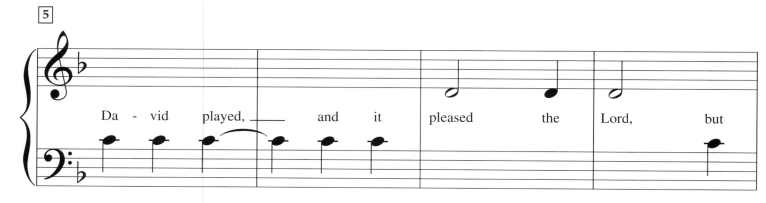

Da - vid played, ____ and it pleased the Lord, but

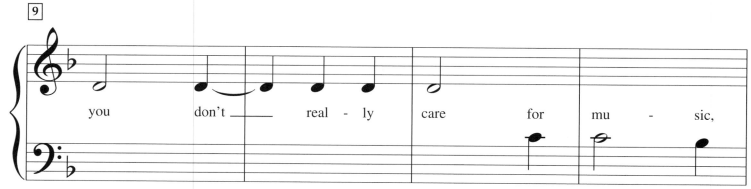

you don't ____ real - ly care for mu - sic,

Duet Part (Student plays one octave higher than written.)

Moving along

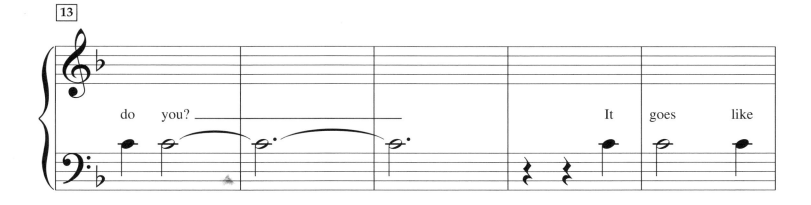

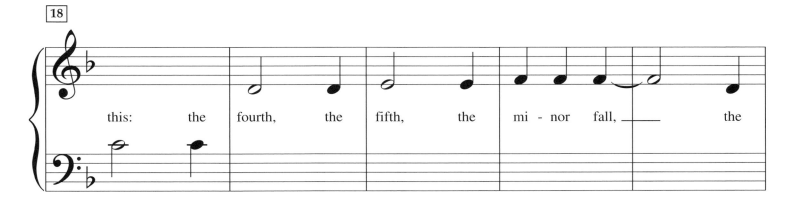

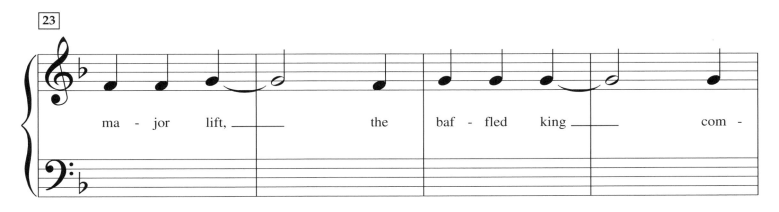

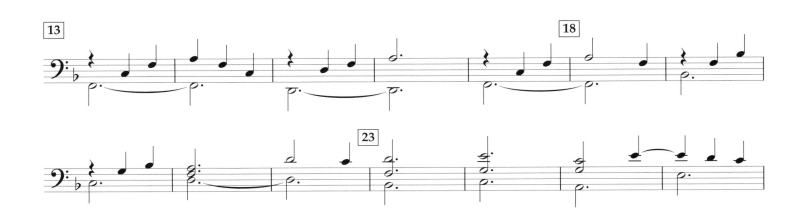

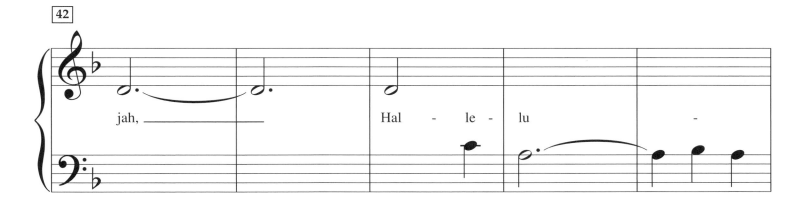

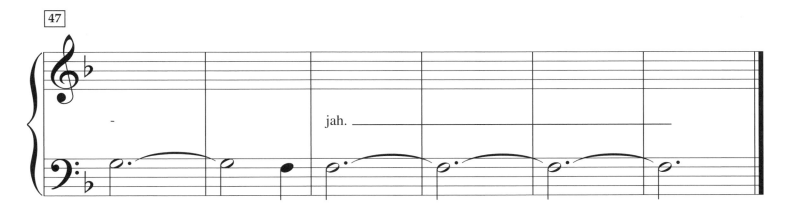

Additional Lyrics

2. Your faith was strong, but you needed proof.
   You saw her bathing on the roof.
   Her beauty and the moonlight overthrew you.
   She tied you to a kitchen chair.
   She broke your throne; she cut your hair.
   And from your lips, she drew the Hallelujah.
   Chorus

3. Maybe I have been here before.
   I know this room; I've walked this floor.
   I used to live alone before I knew you.
   I've seen your flag on the marble arch.
   Love is not a victory march.
   It's a cold and it's a broken Hallelujah.
   Chorus

4. There was a time you let me know
   What's real and going on below.
   But now you never show it to me, do you?
   And remember when I moved in you,
   The holy dark was movin' too,
   And every breath we drew was Hallelujah.
   Chorus

5. Maybe there's a God above,
   And all I ever learned from love
   Was how to shoot at someone who outdrew you.
   And it's not a cry you can hear at night.
   It's not somebody who's seen the light.
   It's a cold and it's a broken Hallelujah.
   Chorus

On Eagle's Wings

Words and Music by
MICHAEL JONCAS

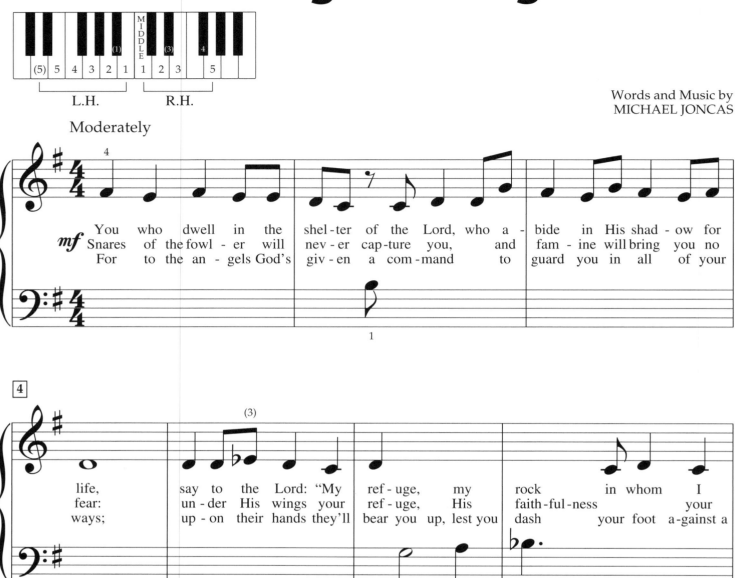

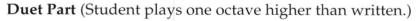

Duet Part (Student plays one octave higher than written.)

One Moment in Time

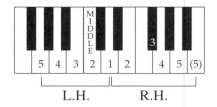

Words and Music by ALBERT HAMMOND
and JOHN BETTIS

Moderately slow

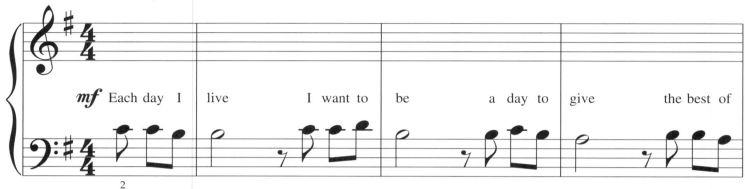

mf Each day I live   I want to   be   a day to   give   the best of

me.   I'm on-ly   one,   but not a - lone.   My fin - est

Duet Part (Student plays one octave higher than written.)

Moderately slow

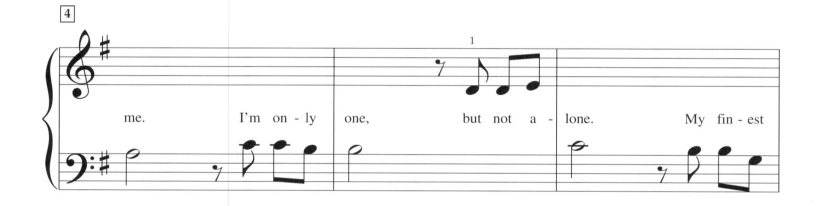

mp
With pedal

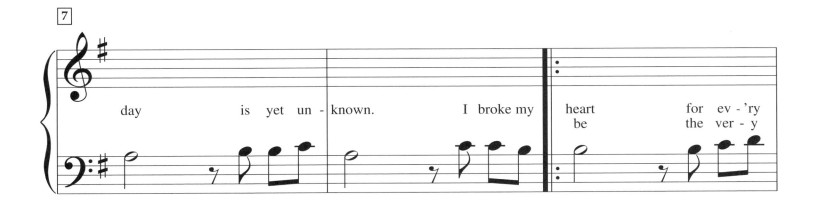

27

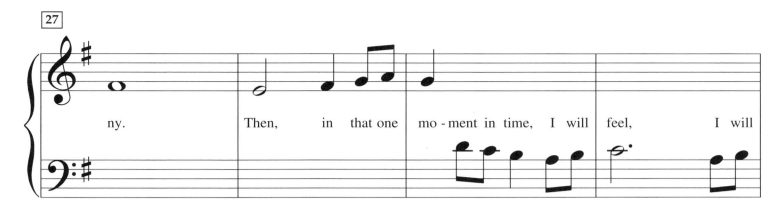

ny.   Then,   in that one   mo - ment in time, I will feel,   I will

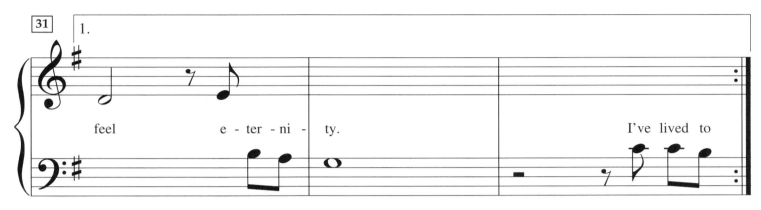

1.

feel   e - ter - ni - ty.   I've lived to

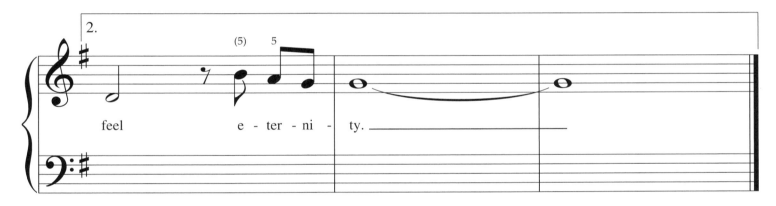

2.

feel   e - ter - ni - ty. _____

The Wind Beneath My Wings

Words and Music by LARRY HENLEY
and JEFF SILBAR

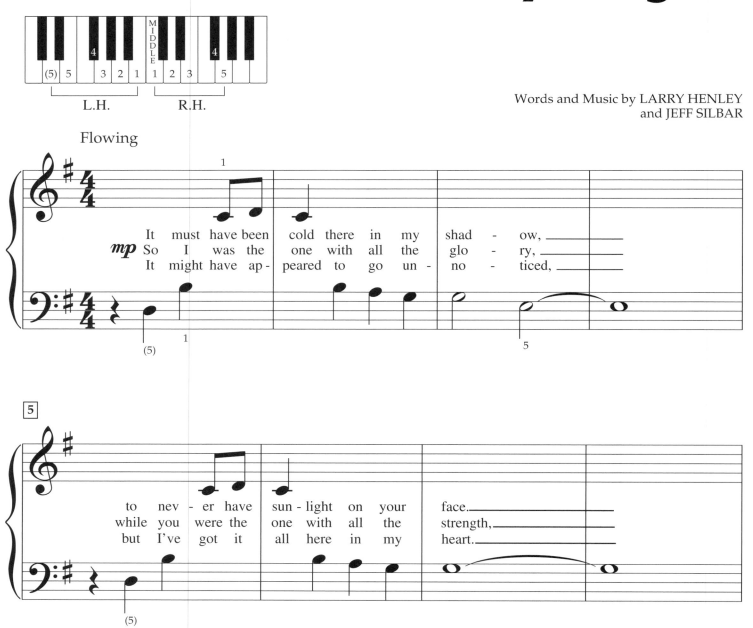

Duet Part (Student plays one octave higher than written.)

You Raise Me Up

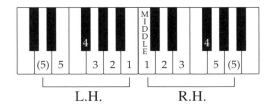

L.H.   R.H.

Words and Music by BRENDAN GRAHAM
and ROLF LOVLAND

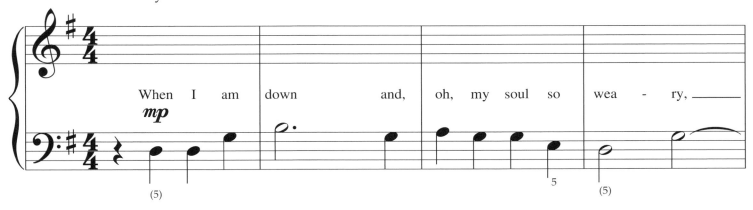

Duet Part (Student plays one octave higher than written.)

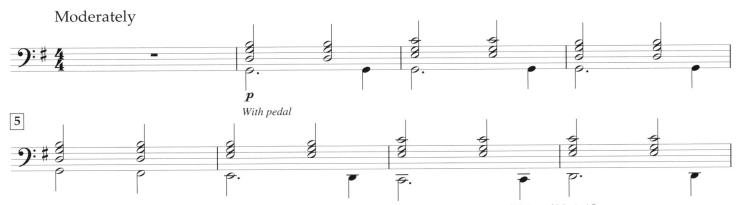

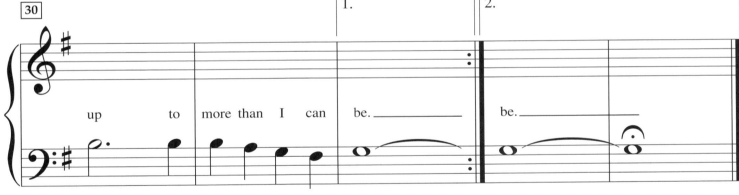

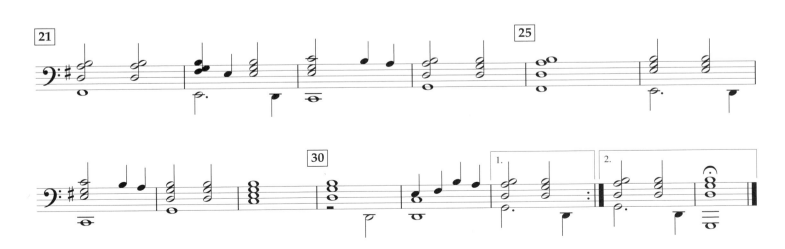

Shower the People

Words and Music by
JAMES TAYLOR

Duet Part (Student plays one octave higher than written.)

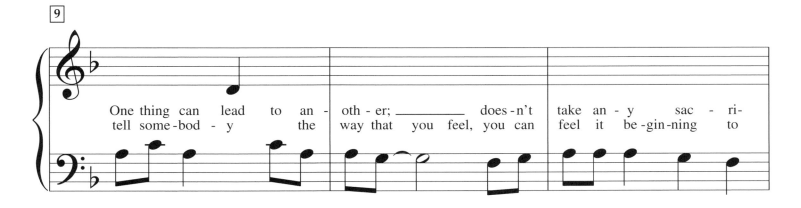

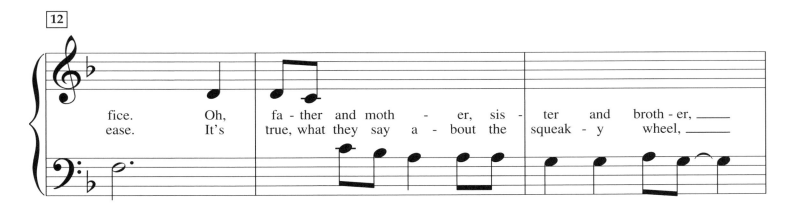

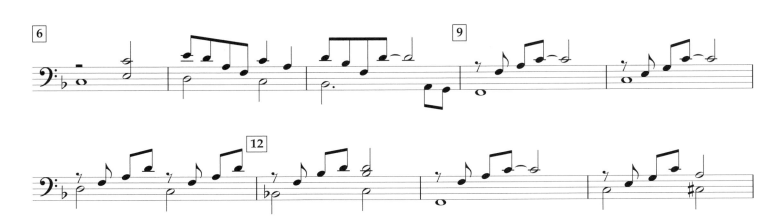

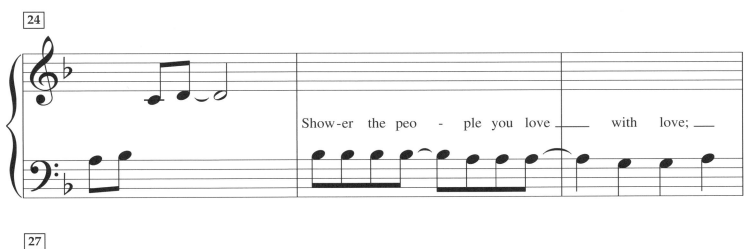